Sprinkle Journal

Brittany Schmidt | sprinklethatsparkle.ca

Content - Brittany Schmidt
Cover Design - Monica Fonesca & Megan Jackson
ISBN Paperback - 978-1-990352-26-3

leadherpublishing.com

leadHer
PUBLISHING

WELCOME

Hey there, new friend! Welcome to the *SPRINKLE: Affirmation & Reflection Journal*. This is a space for you to explore your dreams, desires, and to expand on your mindfulness practice alongside our SPRINKLE Affirmation & Journal Prompt card deck.

Now, you don't *need* the card deck to use this journal, and you don't *need* this journal to use the card deck. They can go together, or stand alone. Personally, I enjoy using them together.

As I started to grow and develop my own personal spiritual practice over the years, I started noticing the kind of impact I was capable of creating if I focused my energy on positivity and gratitude. The affirmations and corresponding journal prompts were created based on my own practice, unpacking my thoughts and laying them out in writing.

Take the time to prioritize this work and I promise you, your life will change, shift and expand in ways you did not even think were possible. I can almost guarantee it.

I am a mother of two beautiful girls who I adore despite how they try my patience! They are fiery and fun and oh so full of life. I am married to a wonderful man and rock. We push each other personally and professionally and work as a team every step of the way.

I love nature, music, yoga and manifestation. One day I would love to be a public speaker and motivational coach to help others realize their magic and watch them spread their wings and fly. I'm so glad you're here!

-Brittany

I AM EVOLVING INTO WHO I WANT TO BE WHILE LOVING WHO I AM

Journal Prompt:

What are the top 10 things that you love about your current self? List 10 amazing things about your ideal version of yourself. Comparing the 2 lists, how can you bridge the gap between who you are now and your ideal self? Are they that far apart?

The next time you are faced with a challenge, ask yourself what the future version of you would do. Start bridging the gap slowly between the 2 versions and watch as your best self emerges with grace.

MY INDIVIDUALITY IS MAGICAL

Journal Prompt:

List 5 times in your life when you felt magical. Share 5 personality traits that you struggle to love about yourself. List all the ways those traits could be viewed as a positive. Think about ways you can use those traits for your betterment.

Often our colourful traits can be viewed as our worst, or they can be viewed as pure magic.

The choice is yours.

REFLECTION ON THE PAST IS KEY TO CREATING MY BEST FUTURE

Journal Prompt:

How often do you reflect on the past? Name 5 recent lessons you've learned and how they will better your future as a result of the experience.

Reflection is important to learn and grow from, getting stuck in the past and repeating negative patterns is not a great use of energy. How will you use what you've learned to create your best life experiences yet?

I MAKE GREAT CHOICES TOWARDS MY BETTERMENT

Journal Prompt:

When met with choices that you need to make, do you often choose the option that is most beneficial to you or more beneficial to others? Why or why not? How does this serve you? What choices can you make today that will help you now and in the future? Why did you pick these options and how will they serve you?

Great choices are easier with practice. How will you continue to make positive choices about your daily life?

I AM FILLED WITH GRATITUDE AND THE STRENGTH TO KEEP GOING

Journal Prompt:

Write about 5 things that you are grateful for. List 5 ways you have shown strength within your life.

Remind yourself that no matter what challenges you face on your path, you have already proven that you have the strength to keep going.

The attitude of gratitude is the difference between a full life and a fulfilled one.

You get to choose.

MY DREAM LIFE IS ONLY A FEW INSPIRED ACTIONS AWAY

Journal Prompt:

Write out what a day in your dream life looks like. Think about actions you will take in your current life that are more aligned with what your dream life looks like.

Does the dream version of you workout daily? Can you implement a few mins per day of exercise? In your ideal world, are you getting hair blow outs and nails done weekly? Could you start doing it monthly to signal your subconscious mind that this is what you are manifesting?

Think about inspired actions you can take now that bring you steps closer to your dream life and watch as the two worlds collide in the best way.

I AM DESERVING SIMPLY FOR BEING ME

Journal Prompt:

Do you show up in your life as someone who feels worthy of their wildest dreams?

Write down all the reasons why you deserve all of your desires. Explain all the reasons why these desires are possible for you. You are a deserving being simply for being you.

Believe it.

I GROW THROUGH TOUGH SITUATIONS

Journal Prompt:

Write about the last tough situation you were in. How did you handle the experience? What did you learn from it? Were you able to navigate the difficulty with ease? How can you utilize this challenge to help you in the future? Is there anything you would have done differently?

You have grown through that situation, and you can grow through whatever comes your way next.

I THRIVE EVERYDAY IN EACH AND EVERY WAY

Journal Prompt:

What does thriving mean to you? How would thriving each day in every way make you feel? What would that look like in your daily life?

Is there a mindfulness habit you can introduce into your routine to get you closer to the thriving version of yourself?

Imagine all the ways you will thrive.

MY LIFE HOLDS LIMITLESS POSSIBILITIES

Journal Prompt:

Imagine all the possibilities that would be available to you if you were a LIMITLESS being not bound by any sort of limitations. What would your life look like? Who would you be? Where would you go? How would you conduct yourself? Can you feel it?

Now remember, you ARE limitless, and all of this is possible for you when you put your mind to it.

I LOVE MYSELF

Journal Prompt:

Journal about all the ways you love yourself and why. How do you feel while you write about it? Are you smiling? How do you show yourself love?

Is it self care, healthy meals, exercise, spa treatments, travelling, time alone?

Remember to always treat yourself like your best friend because you are.

I AM ENOUGH FOREVER AND IN ALL WAYS

Journal Prompt:

Journal about how this card makes you feel. Remember, no matter what is going on in your life, no matter what you've experienced, no matter what you have been through or done to others or perhaps done to yourself, YOU ARE ENOUGH just for BEING YOU.

Keep showing up, you matter.

I WAS BORN TO LOVE THIS LIFE

Journal Prompt:

Journal about everything you love about your life. Past experiences, current ones, and future plans! Hold space in your heart for all that's happened as it brought you here to today.

You are worthy of a life you love. The more you love about your life, the more you will have to love about your life.

Appreciation and gratitude are key factors to living a life you love.

GRATITUDE IS MY WAY OF LIFE

Journal Prompt:

Make a giant list of everything you can think of that you are grateful for. Create a second list of your desires and write them out in a way that makes them already yours from a place of gratitude.

For example: I love my amazing family who I spend quality time with on a regular basis.

Gratitude is a powerful feeling, create the feeling as often as you can by being thankful.

I LOVE WHO I AM AND WHO I AM BECOMING

Journal Prompt:

List all the ways you love yourself. Why do you love these attributes? How do they serve you? When you think about them, how does it make you feel? Meditate on what you've shared and hold space and love for who you are. At the end give yourself a hug.

Write about your meditative experience, what came up for you?

You are amazing and who you are now and who you are becoming are worthy of love.

I AM THE MASTER OF MY MINDSET

Journal Prompt:

You are in full control of your mind and your reactions to the external world. Write about the happenings of your day. Where was your mindset at? Is there a way to improve your self talk? How did you handle situations that came your way? To the best of your ability or did you feel negativity creep in?

Each time a negative thought occurs, acknowledge it and wish it well as you flip the script to self talk that better serves you. Do this exercise as needed and make note of any improvements on how you reacted to external factors.

You are the master of your mind.

MY MIND IS MY GREATEST GIFT AND I USE IT TO CREATE AN AMAZING LIFE

Journal Prompt:

Pick your favourite visualization meditation. Sit in a quiet space and listen to the audio while you breath deeply, in and out.

Think about your best life. What would it look like? Would you work? How many hours a day? Who would be there? Do you see travel, a home, children, fun?

After the meditation, write out what your dream life looks like and imagine all the ways it is.

BOUNDLESS CREATIVITY FLOWS THROUGH ME

Journal Prompt:

Take 10 deep breaths in a quiet space and visualize a vast open space that you can do anything with or in. Write down 5 ideas that make you happy and excited. Why do they make you feel that way? What actions could you take to bring them to fruition? Does writing about them create more ideas and flow?

How will you bring one of these ideas to life? Write up a plan and make it happen. When it does, share the experience in your journal.

I AM GENEROUS WITH MY TIME, ENERGY AND ABUNDANCE

Journal Prompt:

Share various ways you are generous with your time, energy, and abundance. What are your favourite parts about how you share yourself with others?

Describe the most enjoyable moments you've had while sharing your time, energy, and abundance with people and how that made you feel.

I LOOK FOR SMALL MIRACLES IN MY DAILY LIFE

Journal Prompt:

As you set out on your day, make note of all the tiny miracles you come across.

Share 10 reasons why you are grateful that you got to witness them and how witnessing them made you feel. Look again tomorrow and discover that each and every single day is filled with tiny miracles if you look for them.

Where in your daily life are the small miracles?

I AM THRILLED TO RECEIVE LIMITLESS ABUNDANCE

Journal Prompt:

Imagine you receive limitless abundance in every aspect of your life. Love, time, energy, health, and wealth. What does that feel like to you? How can you take action today to let the Universe know that you are ready to receive limitless abundance? Do you have any pre-existing beliefs that are preventing you from accepting abundance?

Dig deep into how you feel about being abundant and what thoughts and triggers come up for you. Acknowledge them and let go of any blocks that came up by flipping the script and writing down all the reasons abundance is possible for you.

ANYTHING IS POSSIBLE AND ACHIEVABLE

Journal Prompt:

List out your WILDEST dreams, let your imagination take you anywhere!

Write out all the reasons these dreams are possible for you.

Describe in detail the feelings you experience as you contemplate how awesome it will be.

Meditate for 10-15 minutes contemplating these dreams.

I AM FILLED WITH ENDLESS CREATIVE POTENTIAL

Journal Prompt:

When do you feel most creative? How do you use your creativity in your life? Many times, creativity stems from thoughts in a peaceful setting and letting the mind wander.

Can you spend more time in nature? Once you start on a creative project, do you feel more inspired? Setting aside time weekly to get creative will provide mental space for more flow and creative genius.

You have endless creative potential.

I AM PROUD OF MY ABILITY TO CONQUER CHALLENGES

Journal Prompt:

Where have you recently been faced with a challenge? How did you handle it? What actions did you take to come up with a solution? Can you use these tactics to meet new challenges head on?

Remember rejection and challenges are redirection. Where is this challenge going to take you that you are meant to go?

You are capable of conquering any challenge.

MY POTENTIAL TO SUCCEED IS INFINITE AND INEVITABLE

Journal Prompt:

What would happen if you approached every situation you are presented with from a place of knowing that you will be successful in your endeavours?

Imagine if you came into each challenge with the mindset that your potential was infinite and succeeding was inevitable for you? How would this mindset shift impact your life and how you handle yourself?

Become the version of you that believes this to your core by practicing it daily.

I AM WORTHY OF FINANCIAL SUCCESS

Journal Prompt:

List all the reasons you are worthy of financial success. You are a limitless being.

Repeat this mantra loudly 5 times:

I AM WORTHY OF FINANCIAL SUCCESS I AM INVITING INFINITE WEALTH MY WAY

Can you feel the difference between the first time you said it to the 5th time?

YOU ARE WORTHY.

I AM PAID WHAT I AM WORTH AND MORE

Journal Prompt:

Have you been contemplating asking for a raise or considering an increase for your services? This is a sign.

Remember, the Universe always aligns us with what is for our greater good. Raising your prices can bring more aligned clientele into your realm.

How amazing would it feel to be paid what you're worth and more while sharing your gifts with those willing to pay for your services? You can start by paying others what they are worth and sending the positive vibes out to the Universe.

Get ready to receive.

MY GOALS ARE ACHIEVED WITH EASE

Journal Prompt:

Describe 5 goals that you'd like to achieve by the end of the year. Create an action plan on what it would take to achieve these goals.

Commit to working through the plan. Put the goals and plan somewhere you'll see often and check in regularly to ensure you stay on track to achieve them.

Once they are achieved, write about how the process made you feel and what you were able to accomplish.

Bask in the ambience of your wins!

FINANCIAL ABUNDANCE FLOWS TO ME LIKE A RIVER

Journal Prompt:

Picture your financial abundance like a long river and instead of moving water, you are moving wealth into your bank account on a consistent basis.

What thoughts come up for you? If they are resistant thoughts, how can you flip the script so that you feel good about receiving abundance? Where do the limiting beliefs stem from? Is there truly evidence that this amount of money isn't possible for you?

What is possible for others, is possible for you.

MONEY COMES TO ME EASILY AND OFTEN

Journal Prompt:

Write out how much money you would like to receive on a regular basis as if you already have it from a place of gratitude.

For example, I am grateful that I receive $5000 on a weekly basis for my talents and skills. I am excited to go to pay for everything I desire with cash. Universe, thank you for your generosity, I appreciate you.

Visualize the feeling you will experience when you receive it.

What thoughts come up?

I AM WORTHY OF MY DESIRES

Journal Prompt:

What are your wildest desires? What feelings do you experience when you think about these desires becoming your reality? Do limiting beliefs come up? What evidence do you have that you're not worthy of your desires?

Write out the reasons you are worthy and reasons this could be possible for you.

MY BODY IS A BEAUTIFUL VESSEL

Journal Prompt:

List all the things you love about your body.

In what way does your body serve you? How do you serve your body? How do you treat yourself? Do you have positive thoughts about your beautiful vessel?

How can you honor your body?

I FUEL MY BODY AND MIND WITH THE BEST ENERGY

Journal Prompt:

In what ways do you fuel your mind and body? Do you take breaks from social media or eat healthy balanced meals?

How do you speak to yourself? With kindness or negativity? Do you sleep and exercise regularly? Do yoga? Meditate?

Try a new way of fueling your mind and body for a week.

DAILY MOVEMENT IS KEY TO A HEALTHY MIND

Journal Prompt:

How will you move your body today? What positive impacts do you feel when you've spent time moving? How can you challenge yourself to move daily for the next week?

A little goes a long way.

I AM A MAGNET TO ALL GOOD THINGS

Journal Prompt:

Have you ever felt like you were a magnet to all good things? Where was your mindset at this time?

Before leaving your bed daily imagine 5 amazing things that could happen for you today.

Pause throughout the day to notice all the good you've experienced.

GRATITUDE ASSISTS IN THE MANIFESTATION OF MY DREAM LIFE

Journal Prompt:

List 10 things that would be present in your dream life. Write about them from a place of gratitude as if they are already yours.

When we write about things from a place of gratitude, we raise our vibration making us a closer vibrational match to our dreams.

THE UNIVERSAL LAW OF RECIPROCATION WORKS IN MY FAVOR

Journal Prompt:

Do you give without the expectation of receiving? Could you be more giving? Share more of your time, energy, work related extras or gifts?

Continue to give without expectation of receiving and watch as the law of reciprocation returns the positive energy to you!

I AM CAPABLE OF CREATING HEALTHY BOUNDARIES

Journal Prompt:

Where in your life do you have boundaries? How do they serve you? Can you think of where you need more boundaries? What impact would new healthy boundaries have on your enjoyment of life?

Saying no is powerful and a complete sentence.

I AM PATIENTLY PAINTING MY IDEAL LIFE

Journal Prompt:

Imagine each brush stroke of a painting as an experience in your life that slowly creates the entire canvas that is your journey.

How do you show patience in your daily life? Where in your life can you slow down and paint your journey with patience? How will showing patience change your desired outcome?

Life is about the journey, not the destination.

I GIVE MYSELF PERMISSION TO DO MORE OF WHAT I LOVE AND LESS OF WHAT I DON'T

Journal Prompt:

What do you enjoy doing that lights you up? How can you bring more of that into your day? What do you dislike doing? How can you remove some of that from your life? How would these changes impact your love of life?

I TRUST IN THE PLAN THE UNIVERSE HAS FOR ME

Journal Prompt:

How often do you get caught up in thoughts about how to control your life? When in your life have things worked out that you didn't think were possible? How can you embody someone who trusts the Universe has a plan?

The Universe always has your back for your highest and greatest good. Let go of the how.

Wait and watch as the Universe delivers.

I CAN SEE THE LIGHT WHEN THERE IS DARK

Journal Prompt:

Picture yourself outside at night under the moon. Everything is dark but you can see a small light in the sky. Imagine a time when you were struggling, what gave you hope that everything would turn out OK?

Journal about this experience and everything it taught you about your ability to handle challenging things. Remember how capable you are the next time something hard comes up in your life and apply these same learnings to that situation.

Can you see the light when there is dark?

SITTING IN STILLNESS CREATES ENERGETIC FLOW

Journal Prompt:

Sit outside in stillness and breath in and out slowly. Contemplate ideas that you have and how they could work out in the best possible way. Do more new and creative ideas show up? Write them down.

Aim to spend 5-10 min per day this week outside contemplating ideas while you sit in silence breathing in and out.

Imagine all that's possible for you.

ONE SMALL SUCCESS FOR MY MIND COULD BE ONE QUANTUM LEAP FOR MY SOUL

Journal Prompt:

When you think positively you raise your vibration that you give out to the world thus attracting the things you want for yourself more easily.

Your thoughts create an energetic field around your body. Raising your vibration can result in quantum leaps for your soul. Visualize your future self and all the things you do in your dream life while meditating. The high vibration from this visualized reality attracts your future self closer to where you are now.

Journal about your experience.

I SHINE BRIGHT EACH AND EVERY DAY

Journal Prompt:

How do you let your light shine on a daily basis? Are you pleasant and friendly at work? Do you share ideas with colleagues and friends or hold space for those around you to share theirs?

Write down 5 ways that you shine your light daily. Share 5 ways you would shine more of your light if you weren't concerned about judgement.

Try those 5 things this week and journal about how it went.

I RELEASE ENERGETIC TIES THAT NO LONGER SERVE ME

Journal Prompt:

Repeat this mantra out loud 3 times, "I release energetic ties that no longer serve me. I take back all the power that others were taking from me with or without my knowledge."

Imagine cutting a rope from all things that you are energetically tied to and imagine a large beam of white light shine through you as your power comes back in full.

What are your initial thoughts and feelings?

EACH MORNING I RISE LIKE THE SUN BRIGHT AND FULL OF ENERGY

Journal Prompt:

When you wake up each morning for the next week repeat the mantra, "Each morning I rise like the sun, bright and full of energy." Repeat it 5 times before you roll out of bed and picture a bright beam of white light from your crown to heels.

How do you feel after a week of trying this exercise? What's different about your day as a result of changing your morning mantra?

How do you feel?

POSITIVITY RADIATES FROM ME LIKE THE SUN RADIATES HEAT

Journal Prompt:

Each time you start to feel your mind creep into a pattern of negative thought, picture your Higher Self lending a helping hand and pulling yourself out of the thought process into a bright, sunny place full of radiant positivity thoughts.

How do you feel at the end of the week? Did others notice? What do you notice about the quality of your thoughts after trying this?

I AM THANKFUL FOR MY INEVITABLE GREATNESS

Journal Prompt:

Everything that you desire is possible for you.

Where in your life have you seen yourself as amazing? Where would you like to improve? Visualize yourself in a world where you are pure greatness. What actions are you taking in that world? How can you implement them into your life right now?

Your greatness is truly inevitable.

EVERYTHING IN LIFE IS AN ENERGETIC EXCHANGE

Journal Prompt:

Where in your life has this affirmation rang true? How do you view the energy you bring to the world?

In what ways are you checking in with your energy? Is there a way you could improve how you show up energetically? What techniques do you use to get yourself in a good mood?

Be conscious of how you exchange energy daily.

I AM A POSITIVITY MAGNET

Journal Prompt:

How do you call positivity into your life on a regular basis?

When you're not feeling wonderful, how do you acknowledge and process those feelings? Holding space for all feelings is important to move through the energy you're experiencing.

By allowing the feelings to exist and pass, you are not held back by emotions that are no longer serving you and magnetize your energy for amazing things.

I AM EXCITED TO WAKE UP EACH DAY

Journal Prompt:

What sorts of activities get you excited about waking up daily? How can you incorporate more of those activities into your daily life?

How would bringing more joy to your life impact the quality of it?

I CALL IN ABUNDANCE IN ALL AREAS OF MY LIFE

Journal Prompt:

What does being abundant mean to you? Where in your life are you calling in more abundance?

Describe the areas of your life where you already feel abundant. Thank the Universe for what you already have.

The Universe will continue to provide more things to be grateful for. Watch it unfold for you.

The Universe has your back.

I CREATE THE RELATIONSHIPS I WANT

Journal Prompt:

What kind of relationships do you want?
What types of relationships do you already have?

Can you bridge the gap between the two?
How can you embody someone who experiences your ideal relationships now?
Create your ideal relationships by design.

Your life is a canvas and you are the artist.

MY SUCCESS IS INEVITABLE AND SUSTAINABLE

Journal Prompt:

Share 5 examples of your success.
Could you replicate these successes by applying the same principles to a current struggle?

Use what you already know and build on the momentum you've set in motion.
Your success in inevitable and sustainable if you believe it to be true.

And so it is.

I RADIATE CONFIDENCE AND MY ENERGY IS CONTAGIOUS

Journal Prompt:

When in your life did you feel confident?
How did you feel and others respond to you?
Can you recreate that feeling of confidence today?

People can feel energy before words are exchanged.

When you radiate confidence, you will draw the right people in. This energy is beautifully contagious.

Sprinkle that sparkle!

I AM INSPIRED AND INSPIRATIONAL

Journal Prompt:

Share a time when you were inspired by someone? What did you gain from the inspirational experience? In what ways have you inspired others in your life? How did that make you feel?

Think about the ways you inspire yourself.

MY LOVE OF LIFE IS LIMITLESS

Journal Prompt:

What 10 things do you love about your life? Why do you love those pieces of your life? How are you feeling as you share them?

Loving what you have aligns you to have more things to love.

I AM CAPABLE OF WHATEVER I PUT MY MIND TO

Journal Prompt:

Share 3 examples of what you achieved that you thought was impossible. How did you make it possible? You've proven you are capable of anything.

Challenge yourself to try something you've previously thought was impossible.

Remember, you can do anything you put your mind to.

MY INTENTIONS COME TO FRUITION RIGHT BEFORE MY EYES

Journal Prompt:

What intentions do you have for this year?
Write them out as if they are already yours.

For example:
I am so grateful that my family and I have health, happiness, and limitless wealth.

Let go of the "how" and watch the magic unfold.

I AM EVOLVING INTO WHO I WANT TO BE WHILE LOVING WHO I AM

Journal Prompt:

What are the top 10 things that you love about your current self? List 10 amazing things about your ideal version of yourself. Comparing the 2 lists, how can you bridge the gap between who you are now and your ideal self? Are they that far apart?

The next time you are faced with a challenge, ask yourself what the future version of you would do. Start bridging the gap slowly between the 2 versions and watch as your best self emerges with grace.

Manufactured by Amazon.ca
Bolton, ON

43082043R00140